Contents

Some words are printed in bold, **like this**. You can find out what they mean on page 30. You can also look in the box at the bottom of the page where they first appear.

Get ready for adventure

Ready for adventure? Planet Earth offers you lots of choices. There are high places and low places. There are wet places and dry places. Where would you like to go?

From space, Earth ▶ looks like a giant ball. Water covers much of its surface. Can you spot high places and wet places from space?

WORLD'S WONDERS

Elizabeth Raum

www.raintreepublishers.co.uk

Visit our website to find out more information about **Raintree** books.

To order:
- ☎ Phone 44 (0) 1865 888112
- 🗎 Send a fax to 44 (0) 1865 314091
- 🖥 Visit the Raintree bookshop at **www.raintreepublishers.co.uk** to browse our catalogue and order online.

First published in Great Britain by Raintree,
Halley Court, Jordan Hill, Oxford OX2 8EJ,
part of Harcourt Education.
Raintree is a registered trademark of Harcourt
Education Ltd.

Editorial: Nancy Dickmann and Catherine Veitch
Design: Michelle Lisseter and Bridge Creative Services
Illustrations: Bridge Creative Services
Picture Research: Hannah Taylor and Rebecca
Sodergren
Production: Camilla Crask

Originated by Modern Age
Printed and bound in China by WKT Company
Limited

10-digit ISBN 1 4062 0485 4 (hardback)
13-digit ISBN 978 1 4062 0485 8 (hardback)
11 10 09 08 07
10 9 8 7 6 5 4 3 2 1

10-digit ISBN 1 4062 0510 9 (paperback)
13-digit ISBN 978 1 4062 0510 7 (paperback)
11 10 09 08 07
10 9 8 7 6 5 4 3 2 1

**British Library Cataloguing in Publication
Data**
Raum, Elizabeth
World's wonders - (Fusion)
551.4'1
A full catalogue record for this book is available from
the British Library.

Acknowledgements
The publishers would like to thank the following for
permission to reproduce photographs: 4 Corners
Picture Agency pp. **10–11**, **14–15**, **22**, **23**, **28 top**, **29
top**; Alamy Images pp. **8–9** (Danita Dellmont);
Corbis pp. **24–25** (Jim Sugar); FLPA p. **13** inset
(Minden Pictures/Norbert Wu); Getty Images pp. **13**
(Photographer's Choice), **29 bottom** (National
Geographic); Lonely Planet Images pp. **17 inset** (Neil
Wilson), **21 inset** (Eddie Brady), **20–21** (Ralph Lee
Hopkins); Photolibrary.com pp. **6–7** (Bildhuset Ab), **7
inset** (Paul Franklin), **16–17** (Index Stock Imagery),
28 bottom (Bildhuset Ab); Science Photo Library pp.
4–5 (Mike Agliolo); Tom Sanders p. **19**.

Cover photograph of Angel Falls reproduced with
permission of Photolibrary.com (Patricio Robles Gil).

Every effort has been made to contact copyright
holders of any material reproduced in this book. Any
omissions will be rectified in subsequent printings if
notice is given to the publishers.

The publishers would like to thank Nancy Harris and
Harold Pratt for their assistance with the preparation
of this book.

Disclaimer
All the Internet addresses (URLs) given in this book
were valid at the time of going to press. However, due
to the dynamic nature of the Internet, some
addresses may have changed, or sites may have
changed or ceased to exist since publication. While
the author and publishers regret any inconvenience
this may cause readers, no responsibility for any
such changes can be accepted by either the author
or the publishers.

It is recommended that adults supervise children on
the Internet.

To help you decide, you will take a jet plane around the world. Your pilot will zoom in close for a good look at the **landforms**. Landforms are special places on Earth's surface. Buckle up! Get ready to take off.

▼ The landforms you will be visiting in this book are all around the world.

Key

■	mountain range
□	desert
■	lowland
—	river
	lake
●	volcano

Climbing the highest mountain

Mountains are high places on Earth's surface. Mt. Everest in Asia (see map on pages 26–27) is the world's highest mountain. Mountains are made of rock. Can you see the rocky cliffs on Mt. Everest?

peak

*Mt. Everest is more ▶ than 8 kilometres (5 miles) high. It takes many days to reach the top (**peak**).*

slope

6

mountain	high place on Earth's surface
peak	top of a mountain
slope	side of a mountain or hill

Climbing Mt. Everest is very dangerous. Climbers must face ice, cold, and many other dangers. The temperature at the top is always below freezing. In January it can drop as low as −60 °C (−76 °F).

The first people to reach the top of Mt. Everest were Edmund Hillary and Tenzing Norgay. They reached the peak on 29 May 1953. Since then, many others have climbed Mt. Everest. But about 200 people have died trying to climb it.

Nepal

Mt. Everest is in the country of Nepal in Asia. Eight of the ten highest mountains in the world are in Nepal.

▲ *Yaks live on Asia's highest mountains.*

Hiking up a smaller mountain

Most mountains belong to **ranges**, or groups. Mt. Washington is part of a range of mountains. They are called the Appalachians. The Appalachians are old mountains in North America. They have been worn down by snow and water. Mt. Washington is only 1,917 metres (6,288 feet) high. It is much easier to climb than Mt. Everest.

Like all mountains, Mt. Washington is made of rock. The rock is mostly hidden deep under soil, grass, and trees.

A day's hike

About 50,000 people climb Mt. Washington every year.

range   group of mountains

▼ *This hiker is climbing Mt. Washington (see map on pages 26–27) in New Hampshire, USA.*

9

Undersea mountains

Even though we cannot see them, there are also mountains under the ocean.

Crossing Earth's deserts

Now you are flying over the Atacama **Desert**. Deserts are dry areas that get very little rain. The Atacama Desert is the driest place on Earth. The Atacama gets less than 1.25 centimetres (half an inch) of rain each year. It is in Chile, a country in South America (see map on pages 26–27).

Brrr!

We often think deserts are hot. But they can also be cold. On a winter's night, the temperature of the Atacama Desert can drop to −2 °C (28.4 °F). That is below freezing (0 °C or 32 °F).

The Atacama is a rocky ▲ desert. You can see the Andes **Mountains** in the distance.

desert   dry region that receives little water

Deserts cover about one-fifth of Earth's surface. Deserts are very interesting. Many people visit them. It is important to take a lot of water when you go to the desert. You need to plan ahead where you will stop for food and petrol. In a desert, towns or shops can be hundreds of kilometres apart.

Crossing the Sahara by camel

All **deserts** are dry. Most get less than 25 centimetres (10 inches) of rain per year. Some deserts are sandy. The Sahara Desert in Africa (see map on pages 26–27) is mostly sand. The Sahara is also the world's biggest desert. It takes many days to cross. Other deserts can be rocky. The Atacama is rocky.

Deserts often look lifeless. But some plants and animals can live in the desert. Camels, lizards, mice, and rats live in the desert. The cactus plant stores water in its waxy leaves to help it survive. After a rainstorm, plants and flowers bloom in the desert.

Travellers are happy to find an **oasis** in the sandy desert. An oasis is a waterhole. Palm trees and tall grasses grow there. People and animals stop at the oasis to drink water.

Sand covers the Sahara ▶ Desert. Can you see the footprints in the sand?

oasis   waterhole in the desert

13

Some people can cross the ▶ desert on camels. It takes a camel a few months to cross the Sahara Desert from north to south.

Sailing on bodies of water

A **river** is a stream of water. Rivers flow across land. Most rivers begin in the **mountains**. They flow downhill towards a **lake** or ocean. The beginning of the river is called its **source**. The place where the river ends is called its **mouth**.

You are now flying over Africa. You can see the winding path of the River Nile (see map on pages 26–27). The River Nile is the longest river in the world. Imagine travelling the Nile in a boat.

The River Nile flows ▶ for 6,736 kilometres (4,184 miles). It flows through nine countries.

lake	body of water surrounded on all sides by land
mouth	where a river flows into a lake or ocean
river	stream of water that flows across land
source	where a river begins

People often live along rivers. They get drinking water from the river. They get water for growing crops. People use rivers to travel from place to place. Rivers are one of our most useful **landforms**.

Sailing the world's largest lakes

A **lake** is a body of water surrounded on all sides by land. Most lakes are **freshwater** lakes. Freshwater lakes get their water from rain or melting snow. People need fresh water to survive. Lakes and **rivers** are the major source of fresh water. Some lakes have a river that flows into one part of the lake. Then the water flows out of another part of the lake.

Some lakes are **saltwater** lakes. Their water is salty. People cannot drink this water. Some fish can survive in salt water. Other fish need fresh water to live.

Lake Superior is the world's ▶ largest freshwater lake (see map on pages 26–27).

fresh water   water that comes from rain or snow
salt water   water that is salty and comes from the ocean

▼ The Caspian Sea is the world's largest lake (see map on pages 26–27).

Jumping off the world's highest waterfall

Waterfalls are places where a **river** or stream spills over a rocky cliff. Waterfalls are often found high in the **mountains**. They can be difficult for people to reach.

Angel Falls (see map on pages 26–27) is in Venezuela: a country in South America. It is the highest waterfall in the world. It drops 807 metres (2,648 feet) into the river below.

Some people try to skydive over waterfalls. Some people go over them in a boat. This is very dangerous. It is much safer to enjoy the beauty of a waterfall from a riverbank.

Tightrope walker

In 1859 a tightrope walker called the Great Blondin crossed Niagara Falls (see map page 26) on a rope. Blondin walked to the middle. He did a back flip. Then he ran the rest of the way. The crowd cheered.

waterfall place where a river or stream spills over a rocky cliff

▲ *This man is base jumping off Angel Falls.*

Exploring the Grand Canyon

A **canyon** is a low-lying area surrounded by cliffs. Canyons are made when a **river erodes** (wears away) the land. Over time, the canyons become deeper and deeper.

Now you are flying over Arizona's Grand Canyon (see map on pages 26–27). It is one of the biggest canyons in the world. Some people go by mule train into the Grand Canyon. They take a narrow path down into the canyon. At the bottom is the Colorado River.

Canyon life

The Grand Canyon is full of life. More than 1,500 types of plants, 355 types of birds, and 89 types of mammals live in the canyon. There are also many reptiles and fish.

The Grand Canyon is ▶ 446 kilometres (277 miles) long. In places it is more than 1.6 kilometres (1 mile) deep.

▲ *A mule train travels into the Grand Canyon.*

Visiting the world's largest islands

An **island** is an area of land completely surrounded by water. There are islands in oceans, **lakes**, and **rivers**. There are islands in all parts of the world.

Greenland is a cold island. ▼
Eighty per cent of the island
is covered with ice.

Green?

Greenland is not really green. Early explorers named the island Greenland so that people would want to settle there.

coast	land that lies near an ocean or lake
island	area of land completely surrounded by water

Islands can be large or small. Some islands are close to the **coast**. Others sit alone in the middle of an ocean.

Greenland is the largest island in the world. It is in the Arctic Ocean. New Guinea is the second-largest island in the world. It is in the Pacific Ocean (see map on pages 26–27).

▼ *New Guinea is warm. It is home to many types of plants, birds, butterflies, and other interesting animals.*

Viewing an active volcano

You are now flying over Hawaii (see map on pages 26–27). Look out the window of the aeroplane. You can see a **volcano**. Volcanoes are cone-shaped hills or **mountains** that **erupt**. When they erupt, hot **lava** flows down the side. This lava can destroy towns and homes. Volcanoes are dangerous.

This volcano is called Kilauea. It erupted 55 times between 1983 and 2005. A volcano that erupts often is called an active volcano. Kilauea is one of the most active volcanoes in the world.

Dormant volcanoes do not erupt often. Mt. St. Helens (see map on pages 26–27), is in the state of Washington, USA. It was dormant for more than 100 years. Then it erupted in 1980. Fifty-seven people were killed when Mt. St. Helens erupted.

dormant	quiet or not active
erupt	burst out
lava	melted rock from a volcano
volcano	cone-shaped hill or mountain that sprays fire and melted rock on to the land

▲ *When Kilauea erupts, it sends fire and sparks high into the air.*

The world's wonders

This map shows only a few of the interesting **landforms** on Earth. You can see **mountains**, **lakes**, and **rivers**. You can see **deserts** and **islands**. The key at the bottom of the map shows how to find the high places. It also shows the low places on Earth. It shows the wet places and the dry places.

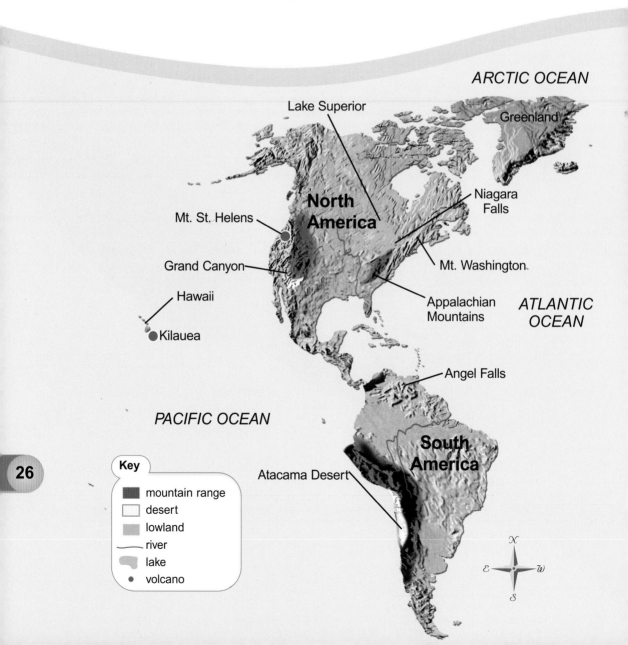

ARCTIC OCEAN

Lake Superior

Greenland

North America

Niagara Falls

Mt. St. Helens

Grand Canyon

Mt. Washington

Hawaii

Appalachian Mountains

ATLANTIC OCEAN

Kilauea

Angel Falls

PACIFIC OCEAN

South America

Atacama Desert

Key

- ▮ mountain range
- ☐ desert
- ▮ lowland
- — river
- ◗ lake
- ● volcano

This trip is over. You can spend your life exploring landforms. As you look at the world near your home, look for landforms. Are there mountains? Rivers? Lakes? Explore them! There is a world of adventure waiting for you.

Under the ocean

*There are also landforms beneath the ocean. You can find mountain **ranges** and **erupting volcanoes** under the oceans.*

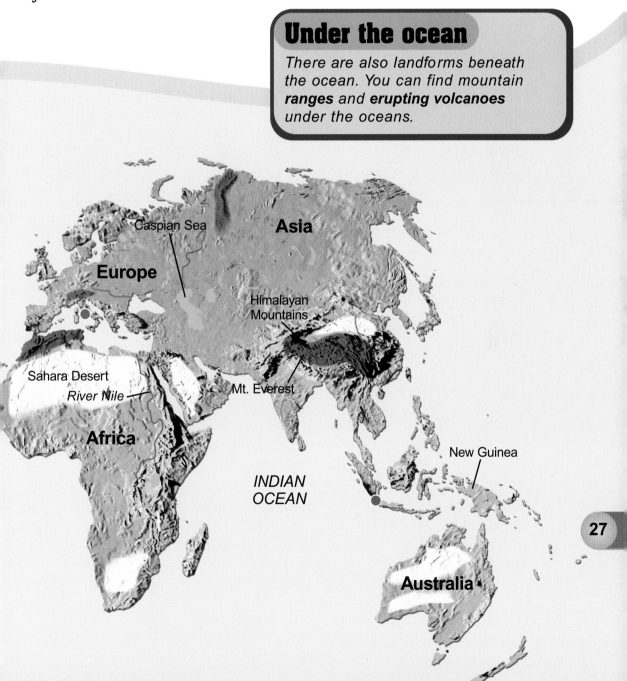

Caspian Sea

Asia

Europe

Himalayan Mountains

Sahara Desert

River Nile

Mt. Everest

Africa

New Guinea

INDIAN OCEAN

Australia

Matching landforms

▼ Read the postcards and match the messages to the landforms listed at the bottom.

Message 1:

We went on a boat today. We fished from the boat and caught two big fish. People waved from the land. Bye for now.

Message 2:

I climbed to the top today. It was hard work. It should be easier going down! It is cold. The view is amazing. Wish you were here.

Message 3:

We left home for the long drive. Dad filled the car with petrol. Mum packed three jugs of water and a picnic for lunch. There were no shops.

Message 4:

I stood at the bottom. I watched the water drop from the high cliff above. The water came down very fast. It made a loud noise.

a. Mountain

b. Waterfall

c. River

d. Desert

Answers:

Message 1 – c

Message 2 – a

Message 3 – d

Message 4 – b

Glossary

canyon low-lying area of land surrounded by cliffs. Rivers flow through canyons.

coast land that lies near an ocean or lake. People like to live on the coast.

desert dry region that receives little water. Take water with you when you visit a desert.

dormant quiet or not active. Dormant volcanoes do not erupt.

erode wear away. Water erodes dry land to make a canyon.

erupt burst out. When volcanoes erupt, dust fills the air.

fresh water water that comes from rain or snow. Fresh water is safe to drink.

island area of land completely surrounded by water. You have to use a bridge or a boat to reach an island.

lake body of water surrounded on all sides by land. Many people enjoy swimming in lakes.

landform special shape on Earth's surface. Mountains are a type of landform.

lava melted rock from a volcano. Lava covers the ground near volcanoes.

mountain high place on Earth's surface. Mountain climbing is a sport.

mouth where a river flows into a lake or ocean. A river is biggest at its mouth.

oasis waterhole in the desert. Palm trees sometimes grow at an oasis.

peak top of a mountain. Also known as a summit.

range group of mountains. The Himalayas are the world's tallest mountain range.

river stream of water that flows across land. Many people fish in rivers.

salt water water that is salty and comes from the ocean. Salt water is not a good source of drinking water.

slope side of a mountain or hill. It can be steep or gentle.

source where a river begins. Most rivers have their source in the mountains.

volcano cone-shaped hill or mountain that sprays fire and melted rock on to the land. A volcano can destroy homes when it erupts.

waterfall place where a river or stream spills over a rocky cliff. Niagara Falls is a waterfall in North America.

Want to know more?

Books to read

- *Explore Geography: Investigating Coasts*, Fred Martin (Heinemann Library, 2006)

- *Habitat Explorer: Mountain Explorer*, Greg Pyers (Raintree, 2004)

- *Landscapes and People: Earth's Changing Rivers*, Neil Morris (Raintree, 2004)

Websites

- http://www.nps.gov/grca/
  Learn more about the Grand Canyon.

- http://volcano.und.nodak.edu/
  Learn about volcanoes and how they work at Volcano World. Click on Kids Door for games and adventures.

- http://www.nationalgeographic.com/kids/
  Play geography games.

Rain, streams, and rivers wear away soil and rocks. To find out how water helps shape the land, read **The Disappearing Mountain and Other Earth Mysteries**.

Find your way around Earth's landforms, cities, and roads in **Lost!** There is a catch. You will just have a few maps, a ruler, and a compass!

Index